THIS BOOK
BELONGS TO

By Order of
Albert Mouse

ALBERT LEARNS TO SWIM

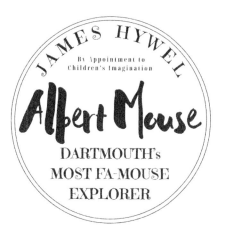

JAMES HYWEL

By Appointment to
Children's Imagination

Albert Mouse

DARTMOUTH's
MOST FA-MOUSE
EXPLORER

Albert learns to swim

The Adventures of Albert Mouse
Book Six

James Hywel

OINK
BOOKS

Written for

Morgan & Josie

and

Mr Spike

Albert Books

The mouse who wanted to see the world

Albert and the smuggler Mickey Mustard

Albert takes to the sky

Albert and the runaway train

Albert buys a boat

Albert learns to swim

Chapter 1

Albert sat on his windowsill, looking out onto the comings and goings of Higher Street. The little mouse sighed and looked very sad indeed.

Even when children stood outside his gate and waved at him, it didn't cheer him up.

Yes, poor little Albert was very sad, and it was all because his mother had said he could only keep his boat if he took swimming lessons.

He had hoped that she would change her mind but as the days passed Albert realised this was never going to happen.

"What am I going to do?" he sighed.

At that moment, Big Tony tapped the window with his beak.

Albert opened the window.

"So, how's my little furry friend this morning?" asked the gull.

"I'm ok, I suppose," sighed Albert.

"Oh dear, that doesn't sound good. Don't tell me, your mother found out about the boat?"

Albert nodded.

"I did tell you, but you wouldn't listen," said Big Tony.

Albert didn't answer, because he knew his friend was right.

"What's the punishment?" asked Big Tony, sitting down next to Albert.

"How do you know there's a punishment?" asked Albert.

"Ha! I remember all the times I messed up when I was young and my mother always had a punishment. Thems the rules of life," said the gull.

"You'll never believe me, even if I told you," sighed the little mouse.

"Then let me guess. Hmmm, let's see. I bet she said you can keep the boat if you go up to the Dartmouth Outdoor Pool and have swimming lessons?"

Albert's mouth dropped wide open with surprise.

"How?! But?!" he stuttered.

"I'm good, aren't I?" said the gull.

"Yes, you are! That's amazing!" replied Albert, looking very impressed.

"Relax! I just met your Mum in the garden and she told me!" chuckled Big Tony.

Albert huffed and folded his arms.

"I suppose she's told everyone in the entire street?" he said, sounding very cross.

"Not quite, but your sister Dorothy has!" laughed the gull. "It's ok, the last I heard the children had started a petition asking for your Mum to allow you to keep the boat."

"Great, but in the meantime, I still have to learn to swim," muttered Albert.

"Swimming is easy, you just float and paddle your feet. Anyway, I've got to go," said Big Tony, and, with that, he launched himself into the air and was gone.

Chapter 2

Albert sat for a few moments. He had the distinct feeling that Big Tony didn't really want to talk about swimming.

"Something is very odd with Big Tony," mused Albert as he went downstairs.

"Mum, I've been thinking," said the little mouse as he walked into the lounge.

"Have you, dear? What about?" asked his mother, putting her knitting down.

"Yes, I've just been chatting with Big Tony...."

"I see, this should be entertaining. Go on," said Mrs Mouse.

"The thing is, do you remember when I was carried off by the wind when I tried to make a balloon? Big Tony said that if you didn't come into this world from an egg and have feathers then you had no right to be flying," said Albert.

"Chickens come from eggs and have feathers and they can't fly," questioned his mother.

"Erm, yes, I know that, but I'm talking about most birds, not including chickens, ostriches or any other flightless bird," said Albert.

"Oh, Albert, please don't tell me that you now want to buy a plane?" sighed his mother.

"No, well, not right now, no. Anyway, my point is that only fish should be allowed to swim," Albert said.

"And dolphins and whales," said Dorothy as she came into the room and sat down next to her mother.

"Yes, and whales and dolphins," agreed Albert.

"And ducks and swans," said Millie, sitting down next to her sister.

"You see, that's my point. I'm a mouse and mice were not born to swim. It's just unnatural, not to mention unhealthy. "

"Unhealthy?" asked his mother.

"Yes, I could catch pneumonia or worse!" said Albert.

"I see," said his mother.

"You do? Phew, I'm so glad. I knew you'd understand if I just had the time to explain the evolution process. I mean, maybe, one day, mice might develop webbed feet and, at that point, then I have no objection to them learning to swim," said Albert looking much happier.

"Oh, yes, I see perfectly. You would rather give the boat back, while you wait for the evolution process to occur and provide you with webbed feet," said Mrs Mouse.

"No! That's not what I'm saying, I just thought I'd explain why this whole swimming thing is really not a good idea," said Albert.

"Albert, it's your choice, learn to swim or no boat and that's that," said his mother.

"But Dorothy and Millie don't have to learn to swim, so why do I?" asked Albert, looking very cross.

"We don't have a boat," said Dorothy, smiling at her brother.

"Oh, this is so unfair," said Albert and, with that, he turned around, went into the garden, and sat down on the bench.

Chapter 3

As Albert sat on the garden bench he realised that he needed some advice from a knowledgeable person.

"Of course!" he said suddenly and leapt off the bench.

"Mum, I'm just going to the bookshop," he shouted, as he climbed over the garden wall and dashed into the bookshop.

Mrs Saunders was arranging some books on the shelf.

"Good morning, Captain Albert," she said.

Albert looked confused.

"You are now the owner of a boat, so I hear. Boat, Captain?" she sighed.

"Oh, yes," said Albert realising what Mrs Saunders meant. "I suppose I am, aren't I? The thing is that's what I need to talk to you about."

"Don't you worry yourself, I have just the book for you, right here," she said reaching to one of the top shelves. "A beginners guide to sailing."

"Thank you, but the thing is I have a slight problem," said the little mouse. "I didn't tell my Mum I'd bought the boat and now I'm in a whole heap of trouble."

"I see, well, if you want my opinion, honesty is always the best policy Albert."

"Yes, I realise that now. Mum says I can keep the boat but only if I learn to swim," said Albert looking troubled. "Just in case the boat sinks or something."

"Well, I suppose she does have a point. The sea can be a very dangerous place if you can't swim," said Mrs Saunders, looking at Albert.

"Can you swim, Mrs Saunders?" asked Albert.

"I certainly can. When I was about your age I used to go up to the outdoor pool every summer," she said, looking thoughtful.

Albert climbed up onto the small stool next to the counter.

"Yes, that's where my Mum says I should go, but I'm a bit scared that people will laugh when they hear I can't swim. I mean, how silly will I look, an explorer who can't swim?" sighed Albert.

"Everyone has to learn sometime. Listen, why don't you have a chat with Mrs Squires up at the pool? Maybe she can let you have swimming lessons very early in the morning before everyone arrives?" suggested Mrs Saunders.

"That would certainly be helpful, I guess," said Albert, feeling a little better about the whole swimming thing. "How long do you think it will take for me to learn?"

Mrs Saunders sat down at her counter and thought for a moment.

"I suspect that someone like you could be swimming in a week."

"A week!" said Albert, looking horrified. "I was hoping to be done in a few hours."

"I think that's a little ambitious," smiled Mrs Saunders. "I'll talk to Mrs Squires and let's arrange for you to go up there. And please don't worry. It's just like riding a bike. In the meantime take this book on sailing."

Albert jumped down off the stool.

"Thank you, Mrs Saunders. I knew you would be of help," he smiled and hurried home with his book under his arm.

Chapter 4

"I'm back!" shouted Albert as he hopped up the steps and into the house.

"How is Mrs Saunders?" asked Albert's mother.

"She's fine. She says there is nothing to worry about and she's actually offered to speak to Mrs Squires at the swimming pool and says I should be swimming in less than a week. Isn't that great?" said Albert as he sat down on the sofa and opened his book.

"Well, I'm glad she has convinced you it's a good idea," said Mrs Mouse.

"Mrs Saunders said that the sea can be a very dangerous place if you can't swim and since I'll probably be going to sea in my boat I've agreed that swimming lessons will be a good idea," said Albert.

"Going to sea?" asked Mrs Mouse, putting her knitting down and looking at her son.

"Oh yes, after all, I think I should do more exploring of the world, especially now that I have a boat," said Albert. "And, anyway, Mrs Saunders has lent me this book on sailing."

"Well, just wait a minute Albert. I think at first you should just potter around the harbour and leave the open sea until you're a bit older," said his mother, looking very worried.

Albert sat for a few moments, then closed the book.

"Maybe I could join the Navy," he said eventually.

"Navy?!" gasped his mother.

"Yes, I think it makes sense, after all, the Britannia Royal Naval College is only up the road. Yes, I'll go and see them and explain that I want to become a Captain. Once they realise I have my own boat I'm sure there won't be a problem."

Albert paused and looked at the clock.

"It's a bit late now but in the morning I will go and see Reg, the rat," said Albert

"Reg?" asked his mother, looking confused.

"Yes, you know, the one with the wooden leg. He spent years at sea. I'll get him to tell me all about it. Then I'll go up to the Naval College," said Albert jumping off the chair.

"Albert!" said his mother sternly.

"Yes, Mum?"

"Swimming first then boats, okay?" said his mother.

"I know, I'm just planning for the future," said Albert. "By the way, did the paper arrive today?"

"Yes, it's on the kitchen table I think," said Mrs Mouse, picking up her knitting.

Albert went into the kitchen and picked up the newspaper before disappearing upstairs to his bedroom.

Chapter 5

In his room, Albert made himself comfortable on his bed, opened the newspaper and began reading the various articles.

Just then there was a tap at his window.

"It's open!" said Albert.

Big Tony gently pulled the window open and stepped inside.

"Albert, can I have a word with you, please?" said the gull.

"Of course," said Albert. "I'm just reading the newspaper. I think a person of my standing needs to keep up with current affairs, especially since I'm going to be joining the Navy."

"The Navy!?" asked Big Tony, with a look of surprise on his face.

"Yes, I've been speaking to Mrs Saunders at the bookshop and she said this swimming thing is as easy as riding a bike, so I've agreed to go up to the outdoor pool and meet Mrs Squires. She's the lady who will be giving me swimming lessons. Once I've learnt to swim, we'll then go up to the Naval College and you and I will join the Navy," said Albert.

"We!?" gasped Big Tony.

"Yes, won't it be great!? We can then go to sea in my boat and explore the world," said Albert. "And don't worry, I've told my Mum and she is completely okay with it. As long as I learn to swim first then she has no problem with me becoming a Captain in the Navy," said the little mouse.

"The thing is Albert, that's what I need to talk to you about," said the gull, looking a bit embarrassed.

"Don't worry, my friend. I don't mean we have to leave this week. I've borrowed a book on sailing from Mrs Saunders. Looking at it, I estimate it will be a few weeks for me to understand all the sailing things. It looks quite complicated," said the little mouse.

"Albert, there's something I need to tell you," said the gull.

But Albert wasn't listening.

"Then there is the Naval College. To be honest, I'm not really sure how long the course is to become a boat Captain but I suspect it isn't too long," said the little mouse. "Anyway, what was it you wanted to tell me?"

Albert looked around but his friend had gone.

"Oh, he's gone. Never mind, it can't have been too important," said Albert and picked up his newspaper again.

Chapter 6

From the kitchen, Mrs Mouse called upstairs to Albert.

"Lunch is ready!"

"Ok, Mum, I'm coming," said the little mouse, folding up the newspaper and going downstairs.

Albert washed his hands in the sink, then sat down at the table.

"I suppose Mum has told you that I'm planning to join the Navy," said Albert, as he placed a napkin on his lap.

"Yes, we've heard and we think it's the silliest idea ever!" laughed Dorothy.

"It's not silly at all. Reg the rat joined the Navy," said Albert as he ate his cheese sandwich.

"What, the rat with the wooden leg? I thought he was a pirate?" asked Millie.

"Pirate or Navy, he still went to sea and that's what I'm going to do," said Albert confidently.

"Mum, may I be excused from the table for a minute?" asked Dorothy.

"Whatever for?" asked her mother.

"I just want to telephone the RNLI and the Coast Guard so they can prepare to rescue Albert, AGAIN!" she giggled.

Albert looked at his sister with a very cross face.

"That is quite enough children," said Mrs Mouse. "If you are not going to be nice to each other then you can just eat your lunch in silence."

Chapter 7

After lunch, Albert went into the lounge and finished reading his newspaper.

"Mum, listen to this! It's written here that a girl in Exeter has just completed twelve challenges to raise money for a children's charity called 'When You Wish Upon a Star'," said Albert.

"Really?" asked Mrs Mouse.

"Yes, let me read it to you. 'Last year when Daisy opened the last door of her advent calendar she asked if she could keep it and reuse it. She then came up with the idea that she could put different challenges behind each door for her to complete daily to raise money for charity. For twenty-five days, Daisy completed one challenge a day', it says."

"Every day?" asked Mrs Mouse.

"That's what it says. The challenges have included a sponsored silence, a thirty-mile bike ride, a litter pick and a two-mile swim!" said Albert.

The little mouse sat back in his chair.

"Wow, can you imagine? A two-mile swim, that's like from here to....."

Albert paused, as he tried to work out how far two miles was.

"It's a jolly long way, that much I do know," he said.

"You should ask her to teach you to swim," said his mother.

The little mouse scratched his chin as he thought about what his mother had said.

"You know what, Mum, that is a brilliant idea!" he said.

"I do have them occasionally," chuckled Mrs Mouse.

Albert folded up the newspaper and jumped off the chair.

"Where are you going now?" asked his mother.

"I'm going to see Mrs Saunders again and see if she will help me donate ten pounds to When You Wish Upon A Star," said Albert. "Then I'm going to come home and write a letter to Daisy and ask her if she will teach me to swim."

"But she lives in Exeter, Albert. That's a long way for her to come just to teach you how to swim."

"It's fine, Mum. If she's cycled thirty miles I'm sure coming to Dartmouth will be easy."

With that, the little mouse went to see Mrs Saunders.

A few minutes later Albert returned.

"All done!' he said.

"I'm very proud of you, donating money like that," said his mother.

"I think that it is what I should do especially now that I'm a celebrity," said Albert getting himself a glass of milk. "Anyway, as you always say, it's never wrong to do the right thing."

"Well, still, it's very kind of you," said his mother.

Albert placed the empty glass in the sink and ran upstairs to write his letter to Daisy.

Chapter 8

Albert opened the drawer of his desk and took out his writing set.

"Dear Daisy. I have just been reading about the challenges that you have completed, especially the two-mile swim. My Mum says I can't keep my boat unless I learn to swim, so, I wonder if you can teach me? There is an outdoor swimming pool where I live so we could train there. I hope you will say yes. Best wishes, Albert."

The little mouse put his pen down and looked at his letter.

Dear Daisy

I have just been reading about the challenges that you have completed, especially the two-mile swim.

My Mum says I can't keep my boat unless I learn to swim, so I wonder if you can teach me?

There is an outdoor swimming pool where I live so we could train there.

I hope you will say yes.

Best wishes

Albert

"Perfect. It's to the point, polite, but not too friendly. I mean, she might not even know who I am," he said.

He folded the letter up and placed it in an envelope. He then stopped with a worried look on his face.

"Oh, I don't know her address," he said to himself.

The little mouse thought for a moment, before scribbling an address on the envelope.

He then ran downstairs.

"I'm just going to the post office to post my letter to Daisy," said Albert as he disappeared out of the door.

In the post office, Albert handed his letter to Mrs Tait, who looked at the envelope.

"Erm, Albert, I think we might need more than 'Daisy, the amazing swimmer, Exeter!' on the envelope. Do you have any other information?"

"No, not really," said Albert shaking his head.

"Well, we can try and see what happens," said Mrs Tait as she put a stamp on the envelope.

"Thank you!" beamed Albert and hurried back home.

Chapter 9

A few days later Albert was sitting on the garden bench reading his book on sailing when there was a voice at the gate.

"Morning Albert, there's a letter here for you," said the postman, waving an envelope in the air.

"It's probably fan mail," said Albert putting the book down on the bench and climbing onto the wall next to the gate.

Albert looked at the envelope and smiled from ear to ear.

"It's postmarked Exeter! It must be from Daisy," he said excitedly, and opened the letter. "It is! Thank you so much."

"My pleasure. It is nice to see you, Albert. I'd better be getting on my way though now," and with that, the postman left the little mouse to finish reading the letter.

After a few moments, Albert jumped into the air and shouted "Yes!" before running into the house.

"Mum! Mum! She's going to teach me to swim!" he shouted, running into the lounge.

"Albert, slow down! Who is going to teach you? Mrs Squires?" asked Mrs Mouse.

"No, Daisy! She's replied to my letter. She's coming to Dartmouth on Saturday!" said Albert, shaking the letter in front of his mother.

"Saturday? But that's tomorrow!" said. his mother getting out of the chair. "I'd better bake a cake. We can't have guests without offering them tea and cake."

"Well, I'm going to tell Big Tony, he'll be so excited," said Albert, running out of the lounge.

"Hang on, Albert. Does Daisy like chocolate cake or Victoria sponge with cream?" asked Mrs Mouse.

Albert thought for a moment.

"Chocolate. Everyone likes chocolate cake," said the little mouse and then ran upstairs to his bedroom.

"Chocolate it is then," said his mother as she went into the kitchen to start baking.

Chapter 10

In his bedroom, Albert opened the window.

"Big Tony, are you there?" he shouted.

The large gull floated off the chimney pot and glided down onto the window ledge.

"Hey Albert, you seemed quite excited outside. Who was the letter from?"

"It's from Daisy, she will be here tomorrow to start my lessons," said Albert waving the letter in his hand.

"Daisy?" asked Big Tony, looking confused.

Albert sighed.

"Don't you remember? The little girl who is a champion long-distance swimmer," said the little mouse looking at his friend. "She is going to teach me to swim."

"Oh, Daisy. Yes, I do remember something about her now. Right, Albert, listen. About this swimming thing, there is something I have to tell you," said the gull.

"Later," said Albert. "You and I need to hurry down to Hip Hip Hooray."

"What for?"

"I was supposed to ask Yvonne if she could make us a swimming costume each but I forgot and Daisy arrives tomorrow," said Albert.

"Us?" said Big Tony.

"Yes. I thought we could have matching costumes. I've drawn a design. Here it is, on this paper," said Albert finding a drawing on his desk.

"Albert?"

"I thought blue and white stripes with......." continued the little mouse

"ALBERT! I can't swim."

Albert looked at his friend.

"What did you just say?" he asked.

"I said I can't swim," said Big Tony, looking embarrassed.

"You can't swim?" asked Albert folding his arms.

The gull shook his head.

"But you are a gull? I thought all gulls swam," said Albert.

"Alright, alright, when my mum sent me off to swimming lessons I used to slope off and go to the local pasty shop and wait for a free meal," said the gull.

"Why have you waited until now to tell me?"

"I've been trying to tell you for days but you always seem too busy to listen," said Big Tony. "I'm really sorry, Albert," said Big Tony. "You won't tell anyone, will you?"

Albert sat down and put his head in his hands.

Suddenly the little mouse looked up.

"What?" asked the gull.

Albert smiled at his friend.

"No. Absolutely no way. I'm not going to learn to swim now at my age!" said Big Tony.

"But it will be perfect. We can learn together, it will be fun," said Albert.

"It won't be fun at all. It will be embarrassing. It will be all over the newspapers, I can see it now. Big Tony, Dartmouth's ducker and diver, can't swim! No Albert, that will not be fun."

"Look if I, Dartmouth's greatest explorer, can learn to swim, then so can you. And, anyway, it will be easier for you," said Albert.

"Easier? How so?"

"You have webbed feet! Come on, it's just a few days," said Albert looking at his friend. "I'll buy you an extra-large fish and chips."

"From the Wheel House?" asked Big Tony.

Albert nodded.

"Ok, but nobody had better find out about this!" said the gull.

The two friends then hurried off to Hip Hip Hooray.

Chapter 11

Albert pushed open the door of Hip Hip Hooray.

"Morning, Yvonne. This is my best friend, Big Tony," said Albert.

"Albert, good to see you again. Big Tony, I've heard so much about you, how are you?" asked Yvonne.

"Me, I'm always good. No problems with me," replied the gull, feeling a bit uneasy.

"So, what can I do for you both?"

"We need to ask you a huge favour if you're not too busy?" said the little mouse. "We wondered if you could make Big Tony and me swimming costumes. The problem is we need them before tomorrow."

"Tomorrow!" said Yvonne, sounding shocked.

"I'm afraid so. I meant to order them before but I've been reading a book on sailing and time sort of ran away from me," said Albert. "I have a design here."

Yvonne looked at the sketch Albert had done and scratched her head.

"It looks quite straightforward and I think I have just the fabric, right here," she said, reaching for some blue and white striped fabric that was on one of the shelves.

"Wow, that's a perfect match!" said Albert excitedly. "Do you think you can have them both done by the end of today?"

"I think so," she said picking up her tape measure. "Let's get you both measured up,"

Soon Yvonne had both Big Tony and Albert measured and began cutting out the fabric.

"What time would you like us to come back?" asked Albert.

"If you wait right here, I should have it all done in a jiffy," said Yvonne, loading the cotton onto the sewing machine.

The two friends kept themselves busy looking at the jars of buttons and the shelves of different coloured wools.

"All done!" announced Yvonne.

"What! You have to be joking?" exclaimed Big Tony.

"See, Big Tony, I told you Yvonne was amazing!" declared Albert.

"Now, let's see if they fit?" said Yvonne. "Who is going first?"

"Me," said Albert, walking into the dressing room with his swimming costume.

A few moments later he reappeared wearing the blue and white costume.

"It's spot on," said Albert, looking pleased with himself. "Your turn, Big Tony."

The gull picked up his costume and went inside the changing room.

"How are you doing in there?" asked Albert after several minutes.

"It makes me look fat!" said Big Tony, from behind the door.

"Let me see," said Albert.

Slowly Big Tony opened the door.

"If you laugh, I'm not going to be happy."

"Oh, it doesn't make you look fat," said Yvonne. "I'd say quite the opposite."

"Really?" asked Big Tony, looking at himself in the mirror.

"Most certainly," said Yvonne.

"I'd agree," said Albert.

"Yes, now I think about it, I do look sort of athletic in it, don't I?" said the gull, admiring himself.

Albert and Big Tony then changed out of their swimming costumes.

"How much do we owe you?" asked Albert.

"Don't be silly. Since you wore the jacket I made you at the Regatta, my sales have doubled with people ordering 'Albert Jackets', so these are my gift to you and it's my pleasure," said Yvonne.

The two friends said goodbye and headed back to Higher Street.

Chapter 12

Back at No.10, Big Tony paused at the gate.

"Remember, Albert, don't say a word to your family about me not being able to swim."

"Don't worry. My lips are sealed," said Albert. "Now don't forget, Daisy will be here tomorrow morning so make sure you're up early and ready. We need to get to the pool before the other people arrive."

"Got it. See you tomorrow," said the gull.

Albert walked up the garden path and opened the front door.

"Mum, I'm home!" he shouted.

"How did you get on with the swimming costume?" asked his mother from the kitchen.

"All done and it's perfect," replied Albert.

"Well, come on, try it on and let's see," said his mother.

"I don't think so, Mum, not in front of my sisters, and, anyway, I tried it on in the shop and it fits just fine. So does Big Tony's," said Albert.

"Oh, Big Tony's going swimming too, is he?" asked Mrs Mouse.

"Erm, yes. Well, just for the exercise. Not for swimming lessons obviously," replied Albert quickly.

"I should think not. After all, he's a gull and they take to the water like.... well, like a gull, I suppose."

"Exactly. Anyway, I'd better take the costumes upstairs. What time is supper?" asked the little mouse.

"Ten minutes, so you have time to wash your hands," said his mother.

Albert hurried upstairs and put the costumes in his wardrobe. He then washed his hands and went downstairs to have his supper.

As the little mouse family ate their food, Mrs Mouse turned to her son.

"You know, I'm very proud of you for agreeing to go for swimming lessons," she said.

"Thanks," replied Albert.

"Well, at least Big Tony will be there to rescue you if you start to sink," giggled Dorothy.

Albert opened his mouth to say something but then remembered the promise he had made to his friend.

"What time is Daisy arriving tomorrow?" asked Millie.

"She said she would be here very early," answered Albert.

"Mum, can I go with Albert to the swimming pool?" asked Millie.

"You'll have to ask your brother, but I don't see any reason why not," said Mrs Mouse.

"I really don't think that is such a good idea!" stuttered Albert.

"Why ever not? I think it's a wonderful idea. Maybe we will all come to the pool, it will be a nice day out," said Albert's mother.

Albert immediately pushed his chair back and stood up.

"No, you can't!" he shouted.

"Can't?" asked his mother looking surprised at her son's outburst.

"No, you have to book in advance and there are no places left," said Albert, looking worried as beads of sweat started to roll down his face.

Mrs Mouse looked at her son.

"Albert, what's going on?" she asked.

"Nothing," said Albert, turning and running upstairs.

"What's wrong with him?" asked Dorothy.

"Maybe your brother feels a little embarrassed with us all watching him while he has his swimming lessons," said Mrs Mouse.

Chapter 13

Albert didn't come out of his room for the rest of the evening and eventually fell asleep.

The next morning the little mouse was woken by some tapping at his window.

"Oh it's you," said Albert opening the window.

"Morning," said Big Tony. "Sorry I'm late, but I just found an extra large pasty down by the quayside and I thought to myself 'I'm going to be having me some of that'. Anyway, are we ready?"

"Yes, but we have a slight problem. My family asked if they could come and watch us at the pool," said Albert.

A look of horror came over the gull's face.

"Don't worry. I made up an excuse and I think it's all okay now," said the little mouse.

"It had better be, because if they're going then I'm not," said the gull.

Just then there was a knock at the gate outside and the gull looked down from the window ledge.

"Is that Daisy?" asked Albert excitedly, dashing out of his bedroom and running downstairs.

By the time he had reached the bottom of the stairs his mother had already opened the gate and was showing Daisy into the house.

"Ah, here he is," said Mrs Mouse. "Daisy, this is my son, Albert."

The little girl knelt down and shook Albert's hand.

"I'm very pleased to meet you, Albert Mouse," she said.

"Hello, Daisy. Please call me Albert. I hope your journey wasn't too bad?"

"Not at all," said Daisy getting to her feet. "So, are you ready?"

"I've not had my breakfast yet," said Albert, looking at his mother.

"The first rule of swimming is you should never swim straight after you've eaten," said Daisy.

"Oh, that might be a problem because Big T....," began Albert, but suddenly paused. "Actually, that's not a problem. I'll have my breakfast when we get back. I'll just go and get my swimming costume."

With that, Albert ran back up the stairs into his bedroom, leaving Daisy with his mother.

"Oh, Mrs Mouse, Albert is delightful. I just want to pick him up and cuddle him," said Daisy.

"Oh, he's delightful," interrupted Dorothy. "You should see the photos of him when he was a baby!"

"Yes, in his nappy," giggled Millie.

A few moments later Albert returned with a small bag.

"Right, I'm ready, let's go!" he said.

Chapter 14

Albert and Daisy ran down the garden.

"Good luck!" shouted Mrs Mouse as they disappeared out through the gate.

Before Albert and Daisy had reached the end of Higher Street, Big Tony swooped down, startling Daisy.

"Oh, go away bird!" she said, waving her arms about.

"It's ok, this is my friend, Big Tony," said Albert smiling.

"Morning, Daisy," the gull said, bowing his head.

"Oh, I'm sorry. I thought you were one of those seagulls like the ones we get at home. You know, the ones who always try to steal your ice cream," said Daisy.

"Big Tony's not like that, are you?" said Albert.

"Oh no, not me. I wouldn't be seen hanging out with those types," he said, putting on a posh voice.

"Well, I'm very pleased to meet you, Big Tony."

"Albert, did you remember to bring my swimming costume?" asked Big Tony in a whisper.

The little mouse nodded and held up the bag.

"Are you going to be swimming with us as well?" asked Daisy.

Albert looked around to make sure no one was listening.

"The thing is, Daisy, Big Tony can't swim either, but we can't tell anyone," whispered Albert.

"I see," Daisy said, looking a bit surprised. "I thought all gulls could swim. Well, I suppose I can teach both of you."

Albert, Big Tony and their new friend chatted as they continued walking through the streets towards the swimming pool.

Chapter 15

Soon they reached the doors of the swimming pool.

"Hello, are you Mrs Squires?" asked Albert when he saw the lady at the entrance.

"I am and you must be Albert Mouse," she replied shaking his hand. "And that means you are Big Tony."

Mrs Squires then looked at the little girl.

"And you must be Daisy," she said shaking the little girl's hand. "Well done on completing all your challenges and raising all that money for charity."

"Thank you," said Daisy. "Some of the challenges were really difficult."

"I bet they were. Anyway, welcome to the Dartmouth Outdoor Pool. Let me show you around," said Mrs Squires. "The pool is twenty-five meters long and the changing rooms are over there."

Albert looked at the pool, then looked worriedly at Big Tony.

"I didn't realise it was so big. The end does look an awfully long way away," he said.

"Don't worry, Albert. We will just start in the shallow end and when you both can swim a width we can then move on to doing a length," said Daisy.

Even the width of the pool looked a long way to Albert and he wondered if maybe this swimming thing wasn't such a good idea after all.

"Right, let's get changed and I'll see you at the poolside," said Daisy.

In the changing room, Albert and Big Tony pulled out their swimming costumes from the bag.

"Albert, are you sure this is a good idea?" asked the gull as he pulled on his costume.

"We don't really have a choice now, Big Tony. Daisy has come all this way and, remember, once we can both swim, then we can go exploring in the boat," said Albert, tucking his tail through the little hole Yvonne had made in the costume. "Ready?"

"Oh yes, just tickety boo," said Big Tony, pulling a face and slipping a life-ring over his head.

Chapter 16

Outside, Daisy was already waiting for them.

"Good, all set?" she asked.

"Kind of," said the little mouse nervously.

"We will start by doing some exercises to warm up," she said. "Let's begin with running on the spot like this."

Albert and Big Tony watched Daisy then began to run on the spot too.

"Now, swing your arms like this," she said.

"Phew, I'm tired already," said Big Tony sounding out of breath. "Maybe I shouldn't have eaten that pasty for breakfast."

"And relax," said Daisy, standing still. "Does that feel better?"

Albert and Big Tony both collapsed on the grass panting.

"Maybe I should have done some training before today," said the little mouse.

"Swimming is very tiring, more tiring than most people think," said Daisy as she went to see Mrs Squires.

She returned with a bucket of water.

"Are we going to start by swimming in that?" asked Albert.

"No, silly. We are going to practice putting our heads underwater and blowing bubbles," replied Daisy.

"Say what!?" asked Big Tony. "I don't think so, I mean, I've never even washed my face!"

"You have to practice feeling comfortable having your head underwater before you can learn to swim and that's the rule," said Daisy.

"Really!?" asked Albert, looking worriedly at the bucket.

"You'll be fine. I'll go first to show you how to do it."

Daisy knelt down and plunged her head into the water. Soon bubbles started to appear on the surface.

The two friends watched and then looked at each other.

"Do you think she's ok? She's been in there quite a while," said Albert.

"Do you want me to drag her out?" asked Big Tony.

Just then, Daisy brought her head out of the bucket and wiped the water from her eyes.

"Right, who's next?' she asked.

Chapter 17

Albert and Big Tony looked at each other.

"You go first," said the gull.

"Oh no, I think you should," said Albert.

"Oh no, I insist, after you," said Big Tony. "It's your boat."

"It's our boat," said the little mouse. "You go first...,"

"Boys!" shouted Daisy, causing the two friends to jump. "Albert, you're next."

"Me? Why me?' asked the mouse.

"Because your name starts with the letter 'A'," she answered.

"Yes, Albert, go on," said Big Tony, slapping his little friend on the back.

Albert pulled himself to the rim of the bucket and looked into the water, which looked even deeper than he thought it would.

"Right, now take a very deep breath, close your eyes and put your face in the water. Then let the air out slowly and make as many bubbles as you can," said Daisy. "I'll be right next to you if anything goes wrong."

"Goes wrong?" asked Albert pulling himself away from the edge of the bucket.

"Nothing's going to go wrong, Albert. What I mean is if you start coughing," said Daisy. "If you do, I'll pull you out."

"Coughing?" asked Albert looking even more worried.

"You'll be fine," chuckled Big Tony. "But if it should all end in disaster, can I have your boat?"

"That's not helping, Big Tony. We need Albert to focus," said Daisy. "Come on, Albert, you can do this!"

Albert leant his head over the water again, took several deep breaths and then closed his eyes.

"Three, two one, GO!" said Daisy.

Albert plunged his head under the water.

Chapter 18

Daisy began to count and waited to see the bubbles, but there weren't any.

Suddenly Albert jerked his head out of the water, spluttering and coughing.

"Are you ok?" asked Big Tony.

But Albert was coughing so much he couldn't answer for several minutes. Eventually, he started to breathe normally.

"How did I do?" he asked, looking at Daisy.

"Rubbish!" said Big Tony, laughing.

"You did great, Albert, don't listen to him. But you didn't make any bubbles," said Daisy. "So, you know what means don't you?"

Albert nodded and held his head over the water again.

"Remember, deep breath and then lots of bubbles!" said Daisy.

Albert took a deep breath, closed his eyes and gave a thumbs-up.

"Go!" said Daisy.

The little mouse plunged his head under the water again. This time a stream of tiny bubbles rose to the surface.

"See, Big Tony, Albert's got the hang of it now. Look at those bubbles," said Daisy, clapping her hands.

She then looked into the bucket.

"Ok, that's enough. Albert? Albert!"

But Albert couldn't hear her.

"Albert!" shouted Daisy, grabbing the little mouse by the back of his costume and pulling him out of the water. "Are you ok?"

"I'm fine. How did I do?" he asked, wiping his eyes and trying to get the water out of his ears.

"Fantastic! You've passed the bubble-bucket course," said Daisy. "Ok, Big

Tony, it's your turn and I don't think you need the life ring for this part."

The gull remove the life ring and walked towards the bucket.

"Just pretend there is a large pasty that's sunk to the bottom," giggled Albert, still trying to get water out of his ears.

Big Tony took several deep breaths and then plunged his head into the water. Almost instantly bubbles rose to the surface.

"How's he doing?" asked Albert looking concerned.

"He's doing great. I'd even say he's taken to it like a duck to water," giggled Daisy.

Big Tony drew his head out of the water and shook it from side to side.

"Well, that was easy," he said, looking pleased with himself. "What's next?"

Chapter 19

Daisy led them over to the side of the pool and climbed down the ladder into the water.

"Swimming is a combination of moving your legs and arms together like this," she said, lowering herself into the water and swimming up and down the pool.

"Looks ok, I suppose," said Albert.

"We are first going to practice floating in the water, then, when you can do that, we're going to move on to floating and moving our arms. Then arms and feet together. Ready?"

The two friends nodded.

"Big Tony, you can go first this time," said Daisy.

The gull shrugged his shoulders and climbed down the steps into the pool.

"Right, now, when you're ready, let go of the ladder and feel yourself float," said Daisy.

Big Tony gradually let go of the metal ladder and looked around.

"That's it, you're floating!" clapped Daisy.

"I am!" said the gull excitedly as he bobbed in the water.

"Now, move your feet," said Daisy.

Big Tony did as he was told and was soon paddling around the pool in circles and then in figures of eight.

"Excellent!" shouted Albert. "You're amazing!"

"Watch this!" said Big Tony, as he paddled backwards, then forwards, then backwards again.

Soon he was swimming round the pool with his head under the water while blowing bubbles.

"He's just showing off now," smiled Daisy. "I guess it's your turn, Albert."

The little mouse climbed down the ladder and then dipped one foot into the water.

"Ooh, it's a bit cold," he said, shivering.

"Come on, Albert, get in. It's lovely in here," shouted Big Tony from the far end of the pool.

"Yes, that's because you have feathers to keep you warm," replied Albert, dipping his foot into the water again.

Slowly the little mouse sank deeper and deeper into the water.

"Good, Albert. Do you feel yourself floating yet?" asked Daisy.

"A little, I guess," he replied, feeling more confident.

"If you feel your back legs wanting to float then let them. Just keep holding on to the ladder.

"I'm floating!" shouted Albert. "Look, Big Tony!"

Cautiously Albert let go of the ladder with one hand, then the other.

"There you go, just relax. Let yourself float for a few moments," said Daisy. "Then when you're ready, move your back legs gently like flippers."

The little mouse floated around the pool for a while, then ever so gently he paddled his feet and felt himself move forward in the water.

Then he paddled his arms and this made him move even faster through the water.

"Albert's swimming! Albert's swimming!" shouted Daisy, clapping her hands. "Look, Mrs Squires, they're swimming!"

Mrs Squires came out of her office and stood at the side of the pool.

"So they are. Well, I never! I thought it would take them at least a week and even then I had my doubts," she said. "Congratulations, Daisy! If you ever want a job as a swimming instructor just let me know."

Soon Albert and Tony had climbed out of the water and were running across the grass and leaping into the water, and back out and back in again.

"Boys, eh?" said Mrs Squires, shaking her head.

Chapter 20

Daisy, Albert and Big Tony splashed about in the pool until Mrs Squires had to open the doors for the public who were now starting to queue up outside.

After the three friends had changed out of their swimming costumes, they thanked Mrs Squires for her help.

"It's Albert and Big Tony!" shouted one child pointing at the two local celebrities.

"Does everyone know you in this town?" asked Daisy.

"I think so," said Albert with a smile as he waved to the children as Mrs Squires opened the door.

Soon Albert and Big Tony were signing autographs for the children and Daisy even signed a few.

"Right, shall we go home and see if my Mum has some hot chocolate for us?" asked Albert.

"Yes, please," said Big Tony rubbing his belly.

They walked back down the hill towards Higher Street.

As Albert opened the gate he heard Dorothy.

"Mum, Daisy's back."

"Please tell me she has Albert with her?" asked Mrs Mouse.

"Yes, Albert and Big Tony," replied Dorothy.

Mrs Mouse got up from her chair and opened the front door.

"I didn't expect you back so soon. How did it go?" she asked, hugging Albert.

"It was brilliant! I stuck my head in a bucket of water and blew bubbles and I wasn't scared at all. I wish you'd been there to see me," said Albert.

"Wow, right under the water?" asked Dorothy.

"Yes, right under and the water went in my ears," giggled Albert.

"I hope they weren't any trouble, Daisy?" said Mrs Mouse.

"Not at all. They were excellent pupils," said Daisy.

"They?" asked Mrs Mouse.

"What I meant was Albert was an excellent pupil. Big Tony could already swim, couldn't you, Big Tony?"

"Oh yes, I've been swimming all my life," said the gull.

"When's the next lesson?" asked Mrs Mouse.

"No, that's it. I can swim," said Albert with a big smile.

"Really, what after just one lesson?" asked his mother, looking at Daisy.

"Albert's right. He doesn't need any more lessons, Mrs Mouse," said Daisy, patting Albert on the head.

"Well I am very impressed but at the same time, a little surprised if I'm honest," said Mrs Mouse, looking suspiciously at Albert.

"I'll tell you what, maybe we can all go up to the pool tomorrow morning and you can see me and Big Tony swimming?" suggested Albert.

"Well, Daisy might not be able to be here tomorrow," said Mrs Mouse looking at Daisy.

"Actually, my parents thought I'd be here at least a week, so I'm more than happy to stay until tomorrow if that's ok with you?"

"Mum, can Daisy stay in our room, please?" begged Dorothy.

"Yes, there's plenty of room," said Millie.

"Well, if that's okay with Daisy," asked Mrs Mouse.

"I'd like that, thank you."

"Okay, well you show Daisy your room while I make some tea," said Mrs Mouse.

"Mum, can we have hot chocolate instead?" asked Albert.

"Ok, hot chocolate for everyone," said Albert's mother. "I think I have some chocolate cake to go with it."

"Yes, please!" said Big Tony, who was already hungry again after all his exercise.

Chapter 21

While Mrs Mouse made six mugs of hot chocolate and cut six slices of cake, Albert and Big Tony hung their swimming costumes on the line to dry.

"Thanks for making me come along for swimming lessons with you," said Big Tony quietly, passing two clothes pegs to Albert.

"I'm glad you were there," said Albert. "I think if I'd been there on my own I may not have even been brave enough to even put my head in the bucket."

"Really? Thanks, mate. We do make a good team, don't we?" said Big Tony.

"We sure do," said Albert, giving his friend a 'high five'.

They then went into the house and sat down at the kitchen table where everyone else was already seated.

"I've been thinking, I might learn to become a lifesaver," said Albert as he took a sip of his hot chocolate.

"Slow down, young man," said his mother. "This morning you couldn't even swim and now you want to save people from drowning? Why don't you leave the life-saving to an expert swimmer like Big Tony?"

"Yes, Albert, listen to your mother," said Big Tony winking at the little mouse.

"Well, I think that lifesaving is an important qualification, just like first-aid," said Daisy.

"Albert and Big Tony saved lots of passengers on a train once," said Millie.

"Really, wow!" said Daisy. "You two are like local superheroes"

"It was nothing really," smiled Albert, eating his chocolate cake.

Just at that moment came a knock at the door.

"Who can that be?' asked Mrs Mouse.

"I'll go," said Albert, scrambling down from the table.

At the door was Mrs Saunders from the bookshop.

"Hello, Albert, I just came round to see how your first swimming lesson went," she said.

"It went very well," said Albert. "I learnt to swim in the first lesson!"

"Wow, that is amazing. Well done, Albert!"

"Thanks. We are just having some cake. Would you like to come in and have a slice? It's chocolate," said the mouse.

"Oh, yes please, but I can't stay too long," Mrs Saunders said stepping in.

"Who is it?" asked Albert's mother from the kitchen.

"It's Mrs Saunders," replied Albert.

"Hello everyone. I hear Albert can now swim?" she said as she came into the kitchen.

"It would appear so," said Mrs Mouse as she cut another slice of cake for Mrs Saunders. "Please do sit down."

"Thanks, but as I said to Albert, I must get back to the shop," she said picking up the cake. "Nice to see you all and congratulations again, Albert. I'm very proud of you."

"Thanks," said Albert walking Mrs Saunders back to the front door.

"Oh, and thank you for the cake," she said as she went down the garden and back to the bookshop.

"Everyone is so nice here, Mrs Mouse," said Daisy, as Albert came back to the table.

"Dartmouth is a lovely place to live, Daisy," said Mrs Mouse. "Anyone for another slice of cake?"

"Yes please!" shouted everyone together.

Chapter 22

After they had finished their cake, Albert and Big Tony took Daisy on a tour of Dartmouth. They showed her the Cherub Inn where Mickey Mustard had been caught by the police. Then they went to see Mrs Saunders at the bookshop, then on to Hip Hip Hooray to say hello to Yvonne.

They then caught the passenger ferry across to Kingswear so Daisy could see 'Goliath' the steam train.

They also stopped in at the Dartmouth Visitor Centre to see Mrs Gunn and then went on to say hello to Mr Britton at the Harbour Office.

The last place they went was to see Albert's boat and he was able to take them all on a tour around the harbour.

By the time they got home, the three friends were quite worn out.

"You are very lucky to live in such an amazing place," said Daisy, as they all sat in the garden.

For the rest of the day, Albert and Big Tony told Daisy about all the adventures they'd had.

"And it all started by climbing that wall?" asked Daisy.

The little mouse nodded.

"Do you think you'll ever stop exploring or having adventures?" she asked.

"Oh, I don't think so. Exploring is in our blood, isn't it, Big Tony?"

"Sure is," agreed his friend.

"Yes, and after all, there is so much more of the world to see," said Albert, already dreaming of where he could go next.

The next morning Mrs Mouse, Dorothy, Millie, Albert, Big Tony and Daisy all went up to the swimming pool. It was the first time Albert's mother and sisters had been outside the gate and they were very excited.

"Don't worry, Mum," said Albert as they walked along Higher Street. "There aren't any vagabonds."

Once they arrived at the swimming pool, Albert introduced everyone to Mrs Squires.

Then Daisy, Big Tony and Albert changed into their swimming costumes and were soon swimming up and down the pool.

"Well, I'll be," said Mrs Mouse with a tear in her eye. "Albert really can swim!"

Later that day, it was time for Daisy to go home.

"Thank you so much for teaching me to swim," said Albert, hugging Daisy.

"It was my pleasure," she said.

"Do come and visit us whenever you like," said Mrs Mouse.

"Yes, you are always welcome to stay," said Millie as she hugged Daisy.

The little girl picked up her bag and walked down to the gate, then gave a last wave and was gone.

"I'm going to miss her," said Albert, as he wiped a tear from his eye.

"I know you are," said his mother as she put her arm around his shoulders. "We all are."

After that, Albert and Big Tony would go up to the swimming pool at least once a week, until the summer was over and the pool closed for another season.

Albert, Big Tony and Daisy stayed the best of friends. Often, as Albert and Big Tony sailed around the harbour, they would chat about the time she had taught them both to swim and giggle as they remembered the bubble-bucket course.

I hope you have enjoyed reading about
my adventures with
Big Tony.
If you come to Dartmouth, please come
and visit my house.
You will probably see me in my
bedroom window.
You can also join The Albert Mouse
Society

Albert

The Albert Mouse Trail

Now you can visit the places that appear in the Albert Mouse books.

Just look for these blue stickers around Dartmouth.

By Appointment to
children's imagination

If you have enjoyed this book, then please take
a minute to leave a review at
www.jameshywel.com

You can also sign up for our blog to receive
updates on new books from James Hywel.
https://jameshywel.com/blog

Thank you, I appreciate your support!

Acknowledgements

I'm grateful to Brian and Pam, the human owners of Cherub Cottage, for sharing their house with Albert and his family.

Thank you to the people of Dartmouth for welcoming me into their vibrant town which holds an abundance of charm and seafaring history.

Thanks to Daisy and her family for being part of Albert's swimming adventures.

Thanks also to Mrs Squires and the Dartmouth Outdoor Pool.

As always I am grateful to "Walter" for sending me the breeze that moves the willows.

About James Hywel

James Hywel is a children's author and creator
of both Mr Milliner and Albert Mouse.

He is a member of The Royal Society of
Literature, The Society of Authors and The
Dartmouth & Kingswear Society.

For more books and updates visit our website:
www.jameshywel.com

Remember to sign up for our blog
https://jameshywel.com/blog
for news, new releases and giveaways.

Printed in Great Britain
by Amazon